AF754022

52 THINGS TO DO INSTEAD OF TEXTING YOUR EX

Quadrille

52 THINGS TO DO INSTEAD OF TEXTING YOUR EX

In a world where we are constantly connected, one of the hardest things about breaking up with someone is just how easy it would be to get in touch with them.

You don't have to go anywhere. You don't have to get out of bed. You don't even have to speak. Most of us spend a significant portion of every day holding a device in our hands that allows us to contact almost anyone, at any time. Gone are the days when getting in touch with an ex meant throwing pebbles at their window, writing a heartfelt letter or standing outside their house holding a boombox in the air. These days, it can be as simple as picking up your mobile and typing out a simple, **'Hey.'**

But just because you can, it doesn't mean you should. I mean, you know that, right? You know you shouldn't text them. I know you shouldn't text them. Literally everyone knows you shouldn't text them. If you are sitting on a packed train reading this, and you say aloud, 'Hi, train full of strangers. Should I text my ex?', they will all shout, **'NO!'**

So, we're clear on that, right?
You shouldn't text them.*

The problem is that even if you accept you shouldn't do it, it's still really tempting, and really bloody easy. Short of throwing your phone into a fountain à la Anne Hathaway (breaking up with an evil boss is still sort of a break-up), it might feel almost impossible to avoid.

That's what this book is for. I have been there, I have done that, I have sent the Text of Unimaginable Regret.

And I have 52 ways to help prevent you from making the same mistake. **Let's get started.**

* If you're still unconvinced on that front, see page 17.

01

Text literally anyone else

Of course you miss your ex, but it could also just be that you're craving connection. When a relationship ends, it can often mean that we're no longer hearing from the person we spoke to most often. Instead of giving in and sending a text to that contact marked with three red flags and the name **'DO NOT TEXT EVER EVER'**, send a message or meme to a friend, colleague or family member. Try choosing someone you haven't spoken to for ages but always mean to reach out to, like an old schoolmate or uni friend. They'll be delighted to hear from you, and you'll get your connection fix.

Don't waste your texts on people who don't deserve them.

02

You've got mail

Get out your craft supplies and make a card for a friend or loved one.

Note: Do NOT make a card for your ex – obvs. The only thing it is ever OK to send them is an anonymous envelope full of glitter.

It doesn't have to be for their birthday or for a special occasion – receiving an expected card 'just because' will make their day. Maybe you could theme it around an inside joke or a special memory the two of you share. Write a thoughtful message explaining what they mean to you, and post it via snail mail. You'll have satisfied that need for connection without reaching for your phone, and the meditative nature of crafting will soothe your nervous system.

03

Spice up your life

It's time to organize your spice rack – or spice drawer, or spice cupboard, or random box of half-full jars of cumin and cardamom.

Take out all the herbs and spices, give the jars a wipe, and chuck out the ones that have gone off. Combine any duplicates (I am willing to bet good money you have at least three open jars of ground coriander. Why is it *always* coriander?). When you're done, arrange all your spice jars by colour or in alphabetical order. If you really want to go all out, decant your spices into matching jars and make handmade labels.

Having a well-organized spice collection is a trait of someone who absolutely has their sh*t together. And do you know what that kind of person **doesn't** do?

That's right, they don't text their ex. Now, how about a korma?

04

Take an everything shower

And I mean **EVERYTHING**. Get out all your favourite lotions, potions, serums and scrubs. Light a candle or twelve, turn on your favourite music loud enough to hear it over the water, and get to work. We're talking hair masks, exfoliating mitts, body oil and pumice stones. Keep going until you are squeaky clean, slippery smooth and smell like a goddamn spa. Your housemates will hate you; your water bill might too. But nothing beats that feeling of being freshly showered, shaved, scrubbed and lotioned. You will feel positively angelic.

05

Colour it in

Remember how absolutely soothing it was to lose yourself in a colouring book as a kid?

Hours could pass, and you'd be there, completely absorbed, trying to stay inside the lines and choose the perfect shade of green for every leaf on each tree. Well, there's no reason that joy has to stay behind in childhood. Treat yourself to a colouring book (there are some absolutely gorgeous adult ones on the market these days, but nobody is judging if you elect to kick it old-school and get one about fairy princesses or farm animals). Buy some beautiful pens or pencils, then get cosy and get colouring. It's deeply satisfying and entirely soul-soothing, and it keeps troublesome texting fingers busy.

06

Dear diary

Some of us are meticulous chroniclers of our daily actions; some of us haven't written in a diary since that purple lockable one you had in year seven where you wrote about wanting to slow-dance with Ben Rogers at the school disco. If you fall into the latter camp, it's time to put pen to paper once more. Get the thoughts out of your head and on to the page. Be honest, be thorough, be as crazy as you want with it. Don't worry about spelling or grammar – this isn't for anybody else. This is for you. You'll soon find that journalling can become a vital tool for navigating daily life and working your way through your break-up.

It helped you get over Ben Rogers, after all.

07

Still tempted? It's time for The List

'No, not The List!' I hear you cry. Well, I'm sorry, but sometimes The List is what's needed. Get out your journal or a piece of paper and make a list of all the reasons why you shouldn't text them. These can be big ones – they broke your heart, they don't appreciate you, there is literally nothing to gain from texting them – or little ones, that actually still feel pretty big. For example, you might feel embarrassed after you do it, you promised your bestie you wouldn't, you'll owe me a cookie (what, you don't remember making that deal?).

The List isn't just about telling yourself not to text them. It's a way to remind yourself of every reason *why* you shouldn't text them. Keep it, read it when you need to, add to it. The List is in charge now.

08

Don't get cross, get cross-stitching

Cross stitch is not just for old ladies at coffee mornings (although tbh, old-lady crafts are always super fun and comforting, so I'm heavily in favour of getting hobby tips from grannies).

The beauty of cross stitch is that it's super simple to learn: you literally. **Just. Stitch. Crosses.**

You can buy simple beginners' kits online that come with the thread, needle, hoop and fabric, and a lot of stores offer playful and contemporary designs. It's not all 'Bless this mess' and 'Home sweet home', although these can bring a certain retro charm to proceedings.

The best thing about cross stitch is that you're creating something tangible, and it's easy to see your progress. Oh, and it keeps your hands busy. You can't text and stitch. You just can't.

AFFIRMATION FOR BUSY HANDS AND A CALM MIND:

Repeat this mantra while cross-stitching, or even try stitching out the words. It's not exactly 'Live, laugh, love', but a physical reminder not to text them could work wonders!

As I stitch,
I make this claim:
I will not text
my former flame.
For peace is sweet
and silence wise
And closure comes
with no reply.

xxx

09

Rearrange to welcome change

Sometimes we need to change things up in order to get a fresh perspective.

Of course, in the movies, the main characters typically respond to a break-up by moving to a new city and starting a new and glamorous life...

...but that isn't always an option in the real world. All the same, you will still benefit from making some changes, and one of the easiest ways to do that is to rearrange your living space. Move your furniture around, add some new throw pillows or a fresh duvet set, swap out your artwork – and DEFINITELY take down any photos of your ex. Find a new set-up that works for you. Changing up your physical environment sends a positive signal to yourself that you're taking control and doing things your way.

10

Buy yourself flowers

Take a leaf out of Miley's book and treat yourself to some blooms. Depending on your budget, you can swing by your local supermarket, indulge in a bespoke bouquet from an upmarket florist, or slip out under cover of darkness to raid your neighbour's tulips.* When you get home, take out a vase (or a glass, or a jam jar, whatever works for you) and spend some time snipping, trimming and arranging your flowers. See how much more satisfying this is? Instead of waiting around hoping that someone else would treat you, you have treated yourself. Buying yourself flowers is a beautiful and fragrant way to show yourself that **you matter** – because you do.

*OK, you probably shouldn't steal from your neighbour, but you get my drift.

Breathe it out

11

Practising mindful breathing techniques can help to calm your mind, lower your heart rate and temper your impulses – perfect for reining in that urge to send a Disaster Text. **BOX BREATHING** is one of the simplest of these, and it requires just enough concentration that it'll take your mind off your phone. Sit comfortably in a chair with your feet on the floor. Close your eyes, if you like. Then, inhale for four counts, hold for four, exhale for four and hold for four. Repeat this pattern for several minutes until you feel calm and in control again.

(This is also a good technique for calming yourself before a big presentation or a meeting with that alarming woman from marketing.)

12

Do a plank

Set a timer for 30 seconds on your phone, then get down into plank position – either high plank, with your arms extended, or a forearm plank, with your forearms on the floor. Engage your core and **HOLD. FIRM.** Do this every time you feel like sending a text you know you shouldn't. Increase the time by 5–10 seconds each day and you'll be amazed by how quickly your strength builds up. Before you know it, you'll have gone a full week without texting your ex, and your abs will be on point.

30
60

Why you want to text them...

(AND WHY YOU PROBABLY SHOULDN'T)

Let's get really clear on something. Wanting to text your ex doesn't make you weak, or pathetic, or desperate. It doesn't mean that you've 'lost' the break-up. (**Spoiler time:** you can't lose at a break-up. You also can't win, despite what those montage sequences in movies where the spurned lover works out a bunch and gets super-hot would have you believe. Break-ups typically suck, for all involved. You don't win, you don't lose. You get through.)

What I mean is, it's natural to want to text your ex. They were part of the fabric of your daily life, whether you were in a long-term, committed partnership or in the early, dizzying stages of falling for each other. If something bad happened at work, or you saw something funny on your commute, chances are that they were the person you would automatically want to tell about it. When that person is gone, there's a hole left behind. And, regardless of whether you were the breaker-upper or the break-upee (sure, those are words), that hole can feel pretty damn scary.

There are plenty of reasons you might want to text your ex – and plenty of reasons why you shouldn't.

FORCE OF HABIT – If they were the person you spoke to most, you might find yourself reaching for your phone out of habit, to ask something mundane about the contents of the fridge, to check on plans for later, to share a silly meme or a cute in-joke. (And, babe, if you catch yourself starting to type, 'I'm on the way home,' only to realize that there's nobody at home waiting – I know. I know how much that hurts. You're going to be OK.)

It can feel jarring as hell to realize that your automatic go-to person isn't there anymore. But you won't serve yourself – or them – by trying to keep that thread open. Maybe, in time, you'll both get to a place where you can share the odd meme or just check in, but that time isn't now. Reach out to a friend instead, and trust that your ex has mates of their own to connect with too.

THINGS LEFT UNSAID – OK, this is a toughie. I don't think I've ever met anyone who has had a thoughtful, considered, calm break-up conversation where both parties felt they were able to say everything they needed to. Break-ups are messy and emotional and they hurt. You might have found yourself freezing in the moment, almost unable to breathe, let alone express yourself. You might have got overwhelmed by all the feelings coursing through you and lost yourself in tears or anger or pleading. You might have gone into the conversation meaning to say certain things, and then found a whole litany of others pouring out of your mouth. It's natural to want a do-over, to want to say just one more

thing. I understand that you probably have at least one shower a week where the water runs cold because you've been in there so long having imaginary conversations with your ex where you get it all out.

But these things rarely go as we hope. They might not react as you want them to – and rehashing it all might leave you feeling wiped out and hurt all over again. It's totally natural that you need to say these things – and you might need to say them over and over. But say them to a friend (a patient friend), say them to a therapist, write them in your journal. If the first conversation didn't go as you'd hoped, it's unlikely future ones will either. And if there really are things you both still need to say to each other, sending an impulsive text essay at 2am is not the way to achieve it.

TRYING TO GET ATTENTION – What's that, babe? You look extra cute tonight, and you've taken a selfie, and you thought you might just send it to them 'accidentally'?

Nope. Absolutely not. You're better than that. Same goes for 'accidental' texts to an imaginary new lover to try and make your ex jealous. Nobody – literally nobody – has ever believed the accidental text excuse. Put. The phone. Down.

The truth is, when you are going through a break-up, you're not just mourning the loss of the life you had together. You're also mourning the future you thought you had – and the person you thought they were. And that's the biggest reason I can give you to not text your ex. They stopped being the person you thought they were – your person – when the two of you went your separate ways. You'd be texting someone who doesn't really exist anymore. You're holding on to the idea of them, and that person is gone. Maybe – profound thought incoming – maybe that person never really existed. Maybe you just really, really wanted them to.

And that's OK – it's **natural**. It can be part of what falling in love is like. But it's time to let go now.

13

Sever those ties

If you feel like you need to draw on the power of the universe to help you in your quest to avoid texting your ex, why not try a cord-cutting ritual?

This is a simple and pleasingly witchy way to sever ties with someone who no longer serves you.

All you'll need is two small pillar candles (you can get small spell candles that are ideal for this), a metal tray or some other fire-safe surface, a piece of string and a lighter or matches.

- Secure the candles a few inches apart on the tray.
- Carefully tie one end of the string around the middle of one candle, and then tie the other end of the string around the other candle.
- Take a moment or two to gather your thoughts, then light both the candles. Sit and watch as the candles burn down, reflecting on why you want to let this person go and bring an end to this sense you have of still being tied to them.
- When the candles have burned down low enough for their flames to reach the string, the string will ignite and burn, severing the tie between you and your ex. Relish this moment.

And it goes without saying, but practise good candle safety. Don't leave the candles unattended, and make sure the burning string falls safely on the metal tray. We're trying to get rid of your troublesome ex, not burn your house down.

14

10 things I love about me

Yep, it's time for another list – but you'll like this one, I promise. Take out your journal or a piece of paper, and make a list of at least ten things you love about yourself. Do not hold back or allow yourself to feel shy. You don't need to show this list to anyone else.

You can write anything you want to. *I love that I have a great sense of humour. I love how thoughtful I am. I love how kindly I treat the people that matter most to me. I love how good I am at baking. I love the colour of my eyes. I love that I can speak three different languages. I love how great my butt looks in my new jeans.**

This exercise is all about loving yourself rather than longing for somebody else to do it. And yes, I've asked you for ten things, but honestly? **You're amazing.** I reckon you could come up with at least thirty. Try it.

*(It really does look great, by the way. Good for you.)

15

Make a vision board

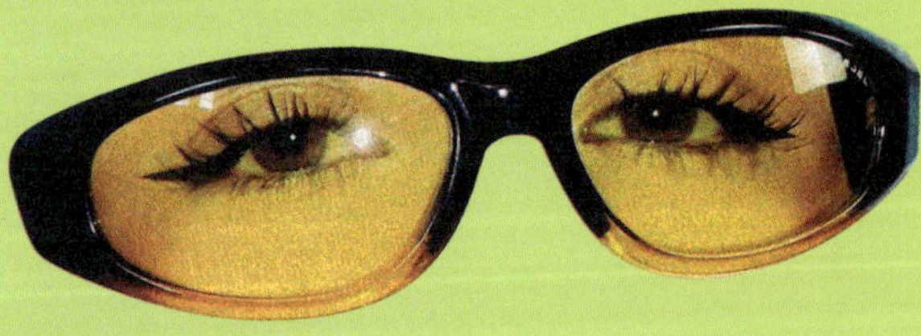

Whether you're a Pinterest person or prefer a more analogue magazines-and-glue kinda vibe, making a vision board can be a great way to focus your attention back on yourself, your goals and your desires.

A lot of people talk about vision boards as something quite mystical that you can use to 'manifest' what you want. If that doesn't really feel like your thing, it doesn't mean you can't still get a lot of joy and satisfaction out of making a vision board. See this as an opportunity to get clear on what you really want – you can get as detailed and granular as you like. So many of us devote our time and energy to other people, and when we come to the end of a relationship, we can feel a bit unmoored, as if we don't really know ourselves anymore. Use this exercise as a way to reconnect with *you*. You're not thinking about what other people want, or what your ex wanted. You're thinking about what you want. Once you get clear on that, you'll start finding your way toward achieving it. We're looking forward, not back.

16

Lights, camera, movie night

One of the best ways to distract yourself from an irksome ex or a too-quiet phone is to watch a movie.

But I'm not talking about throwing something on Netflix on in the background while you doomscroll into oblivion. I'm talking about a full-on movie night – and I mean **really** full on. Draw the curtains, light some candles, pile up blankets and cushions aplenty – hell, make a pillow fort if the mood takes you. Invite some pals over to join you, and choose snacks and drinks to match the vibe – pancakes and margaritas for *Practical Magic*, white Russians for *The Big Lebowski*, delectable cakes for *Marie Antoinette*. Allow yourself to be fully present in the moment. Savour it.

17

Touch grass

Shinrin-yoku, or 'forest-bathing', is the Japanese practice of immersing yourself in nature and using it as a form of meditation and self-care. In its most ideal form, *shinrin-yoku* might involve walking into a forest, finding a beautiful glade and lying back to gaze up at the trees, soaking in the sights and sounds of the natural world, and feeling the earth beneath you. Sounds dreamy, right? Of course, that's not always accessible to all of us, and your version might have to look a bit more like sitting on that patch of grass outside the supermarket on your lunch break. But grass is grass, and while this is a slightly more low-key version of forest-bathing, it will still ground you. Just make sure you choose a patch of greenery that hasn't recently been visited by a dog out for its morning wee.

18

Get thee to a library

Next time you feel a tingling in your texting fingers, make like Rory Gilmore and hit your local bookshop or library. The internet (ironically) is awash with posts, articles and essays decrying the fact that our attention spans are being worn away by a world focused around 30-second videos and AI slop, so now seems like a better time than ever to go fully analogue and embrace one of the oldest pastimes there is: **reading**.

Whether you go for classics, psychological thrillers or fascinating non-fiction, reading makes you sexier, smarter and happier, and I can guarantee that anything you read in a book will be more interesting than whatever sorry message your ex might send.

19

Tackle your junk cupboard

OK, don't try to look all innocent. Everyone has a junk cupboard (or drawer, or box under the bed). Even Monica Geller had one – I know you have one. If you text your ex, you'll be left filled with regret and discomfort. If you clear out your junk cupboard, you'll be left feeling like you've achieved something – and you'll get rid of some excess stuff that's just weighing you down.

Don't be hard on yourself, but try to be strict about it – I promise you that you don't need a carrier bag filled with other carrier bags, a retail box for a phone you don't own anymore or that jumble of mystery cables. It is, of course, impossible not to go on a few side quests when you're clearing out a junk cupboard (trying out all your locks to see what this random key opens; deciding that actually, maybe you shouldn't have given up on roller-skating quite so easily), but try not to get too lost in the weeds. Get out some bin bags for the things you'll chuck and some boxes for the things you decide to donate, put on some tunes and **Marie Kondo that sh*t.**

20

Make a chore jar

Sometimes the impulse to reach out to your ex will come from a desire for connection (in which case, see pages 7 and 9), but sometimes the truth is that it'll just come about because you're bored.

Perhaps you're working from home and things are feeling tedious, or maybe you've got an empty Saturday stretching out ahead of you. The chore jar will save you from boredom-related text mishaps by keeping you busy and removing the need to think.

Get a jar and a bunch of slips of paper. Write down a different chore or task on each one, from the mundane (scrubbing the bathroom) to the I've-always-meant-to-do-that-but-never-got-around-to-it (cleaning your washing-machine filter). Throw in a few treats as well, to keep things interesting. Shake them up and pick at random. Every time you get the urge to text, reach for the jar. Your home will look amazing, you'll feel accomplished and capable and your ex will remain thoroughly untexted.

21

Cookie monster

When you're feeling a little low, eating something sweet and delicious is an instant mood-lifter, but we're after something a little more purposeful than eating ice cream out of the carton in our pyjamas

[though, if you're already doing that – rock on, babe].

Instead, we're going to bake cookies – but let's turn this into a ritual. Take the time to choose a recipe that really appeals to you. Go to the shop and pick out the ingredients. Mix the cookie dough, taking plenty of opportunities to taste it as you go (chef's perks). Then bake the cookies, letting the delicious aroma fill your home. Finally, sit down and enjoy some while they're still warm – and maybe invite a pal over to share in your delicious baked bounty.

AFFIRMATION: FEEL THE BURN, NOT THE YEARN

Maybe your relationship didn't work out, but that doesn't mean *you* can't work out. Repeat these affirmations during a gym session to strengthen your resolve.

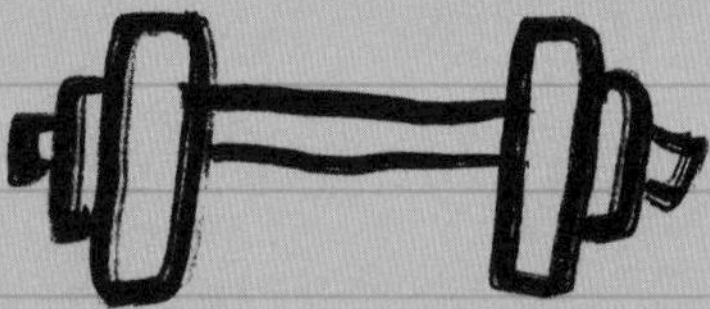

I deadlift weights, I don't lift dead weights.

With each lunge forward I let go of the past.

My body is strong enough to carry me through this.

Stop, drop and squat

22

From improving balance and mobility to strengthening muscles in your legs, butt and core, squats have many benefits – but did you know they can also stop you from making terrible mistakes? OK, maybe not actually, but hear me out. Every time you want to text your ex, stop – whatever you're doing, wherever you are – and give me 25 squats. You might get some weird looks on the tube or in the checkout line at the supermarket, but who cares? Channel all that anxious should-I-text-them energy into movement and use the time it takes to complete the squats to remind yourself of why you don't want to send that message (perhaps you should also consult The List – see page 17).

Seriously, your future self will thank you (and so will your glutes!).

23

Plan a dinner party of dreams

Having friends over for dinner is always a wholesome and comforting way to spend an evening, but this time, rather than just boiling some pasta and opening a packet of Jelly Babies for dessert, try doing something a little fancier.

Choose a date and invite a few of your favourite people. Then spend some time planning the evening – the planning is part of the fun, so enjoy it. Maybe you'll think of a theme and plan the decorations and menu around it, like an Italian feast or a murder-mystery themed evening. Ask your guests to dress up, and get your space looking beautiful. Decorate the table with candles and flowers, but don't worry if you don't have enough chairs/cutlery/crockery. People will be happy to bring extra bits, and a little mismatched charm will only make things look even dreamier. Start the evening with cocktails and canapes (cocktail sausages are absolutely canapes, so don't let anyone tell you they're not), and lean in to being the best host on the planet.

24

Take a solo café date

Sometimes, doing stuff on your own can feel a bit intimidating, especially if you're used to doing things with a certain someone. But once you give it a try, you may well find that solo dates are far more fun than you'd ever imagined. Eventually, you might build up to going out to dinner alone, or taking a very chic solo turn around an art gallery, but for now we're starting small with a coffee date.

Wear a cute outfit, walk to your favourite coffee shop and enjoy a coffee alone – and maybe a cinnamon bun or two. Look **beautiful** and **mysterious**. You may wish to take a book or newspaper to read, but keep things analogue and resist the urge to hide behind your phone. We're all too used to picking up our devices as soon as we feel a little bored or uncomfortable, but it's a good habit to train yourself out of – especially because your phone is currently a **Very Dangerous Device**. Leave it in your bag (or better yet, at home), and commit to being an intriguing stranger in a coffee shop.

Romanticize your life

OK, don't let the heading fool you. I know that we're dealing with a break-up here, and I promise I'm not being insensitive by bringing in the idea of romance.

The truth is that something being 'romantic' doesn't have to mean an intimate relationship or hot date is involved. In fact, there's no reason for another person to be there at all. We're talking about *romanticizing*, and that means noticing and appreciating the beauty in little everyday moments, finding ways to make the mundane feel magical, and giving even the dullest of tasks their own special spin.

Consider the ideal romantic date: a candlelit dinner, soft music, flowers on the table, a pretty dress, a moonlit walk. These are the little things that make it romantic – and you can do all of these things without being on a date. You can do all of them on your own. You can do all of them on a rainy Tuesday (though, depending on cloud cover, you may not see much of the moon). **There is nothing to stop you** from lighting a candle and playing soft music while you eat your dinner at home tonight. It doesn't matter if you're eating delectable sushi or an equally delectable cheese-and-pickle sandwich. Give each moment the magic it deserves.

Spray on perfume before you go to bed. Wear lipstick even if you're not leaving the house. Replace your tatty old dressing gown with a silky robe. Chop the ingredients for your dinner slowly, with a breeze softly blowing through the window and jazz trickling from the speakers. Wear something that is completely impractical but gorgeous. Take a minute to look at and appreciate the swirl on the top of your latte before you drink it. Write a shopping list in juicy purple ink. Eat your favourite sweets from when you were a kid. Dress up to go to the supermarket. Turn off the big light and enjoy the ambience of lamps. Pick flowers. Make a one-person picnic and sit in the park. Put out food for the birds on your balcony. Listen to

Studio Ghibli soundtracks while you clean your flat. Browse the bookshelves in your local charity shop and select a fat tome of poetry, then read one every morning. Use the same book to press flowers. Try writing with a fountain pen. Change your sheets and go to bed early in the crisp, clean cotton. Notice what phase the moon is in. Eat jam and toast in bed with the curtains open to the morning light. Apply your skincare as if you are Cleopatra going through her beauty routine. Buy a teapot and looseleaf tea. Buy a damn milk jug. Make everything into a ritual.

Let the little moments that make up your day feel special and important, because you are special and important. Realize how full and beautiful your life can be – **just as it is.**

(And if you do all this, you really won't have time to text anybody, let alone your basic ex.)

25

Try out life drawing

Whether you've always been a keen artist or you haven't done much beyond doodling in the margins since secondary school, drawing can be a meditative and absorbing hobby. Many great artists hone their skills through life drawing, which involves sitting in a room with a (usually naked) person and trying to capture the essence of them on paper.

Search online for a life-drawing class near you and go along – ask a friend to come with you if you feel shy. There is something simultaneously liberating and intimate about sharing a space with people you don't know and understanding the human body from an artistic perspective. And, as an added bonus, nothing will distract you from thoughts of your ex more effectively than trying to get the perfect shading for a stranger's underboob.

26

Go for a run

I know you don't want to go for a run. I get it. I'm not entirely convinced anyone in the history of the world has ever actually *wanted* to go for a run, except maybe Usain Bolt.

But once you've done it – in fact, once you've *started* doing it – it will help. Just don't let yourself think about whether or not you feel like it. Don't worry about how you'll look or how out of breath you might get. Definitely don't let yourself think about how cold/hot/rainy it is out there. Get your trainers on, strap on a good supportive sports bra if you are in possession of breasts, and get out there. The endorphins will start flowing, and before long you'll feel amazing.

Do the charity-shop challenge

27

Set yourselves a small budget, head to a charity shop with a friend and buy each other a whole outfit. If you like, you can set a theme: wedding guests gone wild, Y2K, knitwear only, corporate away day. Take your time and be as silly as you like.

Make your purchases, then put on your new outfits and enjoy an evening out. Extra points if you adopt characters based on the clothes you're wearing: Jasmine, a bridesmaid who has snuck out of the wedding reception because she's in love with the groom; Mark From Sales, who got separated from the rest of the group on a team-building scavenger hunt.

At worst, you'll have a giggle. At best, you might discover a whole new style avenue you'd never thought of exploring.

28

Dancing queen

When you're feeling low and tempted to send a Text Message of Doom [or even just a casual 'wyd?'], a bedroom dance party is the perfect antidote.

Instead of using your phone to blow up your life, make a playlist of your favourite tunes. Choose upbeat songs only – this is all about shaking it off, not wallowing. Then turn up the volume and go wild with a one-person dance-off. Get nostalgic and grab a hairbrush for a mic while you sing in front of the mirror; try out the latest TikTok dance trend; give it your all with a solo macarena. Within a couple of songs, you'll feel lighter and more hopeful.

29

Start a junk journal

Junk journalling is all about romanticizing the mundane and making even apparently meaningless scraps into something special. Start collecting things like tickets, receipts, sugar packets and wristbands, then pick an empty notebook (I know you have at least one kicking around), get out your glue and **get sticking**. You could create spreads devoted to particular days out, holidays or seasons changing. Press and dry flowers, ask friends to scribble their names on a napkin at dinners out, dive into a photobooth with pals or pick up pretty packaging. One person's trash is another person's junk journal treasure.

Organize your wardrobe

30

If you still fantasize about Cher Horowitz's utterly dreamy closet in *Clueless*, this one's for you. Most of us have wardrobes and clothes drawers stuffed with things we've never worn or can't even remember buying, while we recycle the same few outfits over and over. So, take everything out – and I mean *everything* – and work your way through the pile. Set up a mirror so you can try things on as you go. Make a pile of rejected clothing to donate or sell, then review your remaining items. Hopefully you'll have found a few gems hidden away that you'd forgotten about (it's like free shopping!). Try to curate your remaining pieces into different outfits; looking at everything together will help you work out what works best. When you're happy, hang everything back up (you could even treat yourself to a new set of matching hangers if you feel so inclined), and arrange them in a way that makes sense to you, whether that's by colour, occasion or style. Return to your wardrobe frequently throughout the day to marvel smugly at its new neatness.

31

Get a manicure

Whether you're an understated French manicure kind of person or fully committed to Cynthia Erivo-style bejewelled talons, going to get your nails done is an excellent distraction technique. Find a local nail salon, peruse their colours and styles and treat yourself.

And remember, manicures are for everyone, regardless of gender or style. You might not want glittery gel or vixen-red claws, but everyone can benefit from getting their nails neatly filed, trimmed and spruced. After an hour or so in the salon chair, you'll look put together and stylish – and **you can't text** when you're getting your nails done.

AFFIRMATIONS FOR A FRESH START

Repeat these when you need an emotional, physical or digital spring clean.

As I release clutter, I let go of emotional weight.

Clearing space invites new energy in.

I choose to make room for what matters now.

32

Clear out your inbox

If your hands are itching to be on your phone, then put them to good use. Keep well away from your messaging apps, and spend some time in the depths of your email inbox. Unsubscribe from marketing emails, report spam, archive the important things, reply to that message from your aunt from three months ago (whoops), and delete, delete, delete. Reaching actual inbox zero may only be for productivity gurus who talk about things like habit-stacking and deep work (and more power to them), but even if you just shed some of the excess noise, you'll feel clearer, calmer and more capable.

Note: Do **NOT** let me catch you emailing your ex.

33

Find your signature scent

There is something so chic about the idea of a signature scent – remember Marilyn Monroe declaring that the only thing she wore to bed was Chanel N°5?

In reality, though, most of us have dozens of dusty half-used fragrance or aftershave bottles and no real idea what suits us. Head out to a perfumier or three, armed with a stack of paper strips and a bag of coffee beans to neutralize your nose between sniffs. Start out by spraying different fragrances on the paper strips to get a sense of what kind you like, and pay attention to the styles – are you drawn to something sultry and smoky, or gourmand and sweet? When you've narrowed it down, spray some of your chosen perfume on to your wrist or neck, then go and do something else for a few hours to let the scent settle on your skin. If it still smells amazing later, you've found your fragrance.

You smell wonderful, you've spent your day with intention, and no dubious messages have been written.

34

Groom yourself

This is part distraction technique, part glow-up, part body admin.

When that little voice in your head pipes up with **'I just want to check in and see how they're doing,'** it's time to get grooming. Pluck your eyebrows, trim your beard, floss your teeth, straighten or curl your hair. It will keep your hands busy and give your mind something to focus on – with the added bonus that you will feel very dapper, together and on top of things.

Do 50 star jumps

35

If squats aren't your thing (see page 49) and planks leave you cold (see page 26), then don't think you've managed to wriggle out of movement. I order you to complete fifty star jumps – stat. Your downstairs neighbours might not like it, but it'll stop the texting urge.

After all, exercise is the best way to *exorcize* (I'm not saying your ex is a demon, but I'm not *not* saying that either).

36

Have an at-home spa day

A little self-indulgence and pampering can lift you out of a gloomy place, so treat yourself as you deserve to be treated, and give yourself an at-home spa day. We're talking bubble bath, fluffy robes, aromatherapy oils, face masks, hair treatments, little cucumber slices on your eyes – the whole nine yards. Stay in a bathrobe all day, pour yourself a glass of bubbles at lunchtime, put on some whale sounds and lie back. **You deserve this.**

37 Hold a screen-free supper

If you don't have the time, bandwidth or resources for a full-on dinner party (see pages 50–51), invite pals over for a simple meal – with a digital detox twist. Before your guests arrive, inform them that everyone attending has to hand in their phone at the start of the evening, and that these will be kept locked away until the night is over. The food can be as simple as you like (everyone likes pesto pasta or frozen pizza), and nobody needs to dress up or try to impress. This is all about being physically and emotionally present with each other, with no phubbing (ignoring other people in favour of your phone) allowed. If you want to really lean in to the analogue vibes, use a polaroid camera to capture some key moments of the evening, and listen to music using a record player or CD player (remember CDs?!). One of the best bits will be that arguments (ahem, polite discussions) cannot be settled by Google – you'll have to remember the name of that movie/actor/pop star all by yourself. The very best bit will be that your phone is safely locked out of harm's way, and you're having a gorgeous night with your pals.

38

Roll the dice

One of the best ex-distraction techniques/ phone-free activities is playing an old-school board game with mates. Crack out *Monopoly*, get your detective hat on with *Cluedo*, or indulge in a good old-fashioned round of *Guess Who?*. You can, of course, opt for a newer game if you prefer, but picking something a little more retro has the added benefit of a nostalgia hit. Put your device in another room,* dust off the *Trivial Pursuit* and roll those dice.

Besides, we both know your ex was crap at *Scrabble*.

* The only exception to the phone-free rule here is *Dream Phone*. *Dream Phone* is not banned. In fact, it is actively encouraged.

39

Shake it up

There is something very chic about just knowing how to make a French 75, or a negroni, or an espresso martini. To be honest, most people will be impressed if you mix them a half-decent G&T. So take a little time to learn how to make a signature cocktail or mocktail. Either go to a cocktail-making masterclass or research a few different recipes, then get yourself a cocktail shaker and the required ingredients, and get mixing. Test it out on your friends, make micro adjustments, and perfect every step. Get good at it – really good. You will be the most popular person at any party you go to (as long as you remember to bring all your mixology bits with you everywhere you go).

40

Laundry day

You know that pile of clothes you move from your bed to your desk chair and then back again every morning and evening? The time has come: it is Laundry Day.

Wash your clothes. Hang them up. When they're dry, fold them. Put them away. If you really want to go all out, you could iron them (does anyone own an iron anymore?).

Congratulations: you are not the kind of person who rots in bed, scrolling through their ex's Instagram and wearing Wednesday pants on a Saturday. You are a goddamn legend with matching socks and a clean T-shirt.

41 Ice, ice baby

If you feel the ice melting on your resolve to freeze out your ex, turn your attention to a different type of ice. **Empty out your fridge and freezer.** Put anything you want to keep in a cool box, and turn off the freezer so it can defrost. While you wait, get rid of anything that has grown mould or developed sentience (you're worried AI is going to take over the world, but I'm pretty sure that four-month-old strawberry yogurt is planning to run for president soon). Be a grown-up and clean and recycle any discarded containers. The planet is dying; you can at least wash out a jam jar.

When you're done, clean both the fridge and freezer with a cloth and soapy water until everything is spick and span. Return any food that hasn't become a biohazard to its rightful place, arranged in a pleasing manner. Feel smug.

42

10-minute clear-out

This is sort of the opposite of a supermarket sweep, and it's a great way to expend the nervous energy that might otherwise turn into sending a **Regrettable Message**. Set yourself a timer for 10 minutes, grab a bin bag, and storm around your room or your flat like a person possessed, searching for items to declutter. The speed element is great here, as it stops you second-guessing yourself. However, this does come with the caveat that you shouldn't throw out things that belong to other people – and the 10-minute declutter probably isn't the time to make big decisions about family heirlooms. We're really looking for tat here – that pile of junk mail that's been sitting on the coffee table for two weeks, the cup full of dried-out biros, that weirdly massive free mug you were sent when you bought a new sports bra. Clear it out and clear your mind.

43

OK, you can write the message*

But you absolutely bloody cannot send it. If you really feel like you need to get something off your chest, write it down.

But – and I cannot stress this enough – **DO NOT PRESS SEND**. For safety's sake, do it in your Notes app rather than in the message thread, just in case your thumb slips. And the very trigger-happy among you are hereby banned from drafting the message on your phones full stop. You are relegated to scrap paper or your journal.

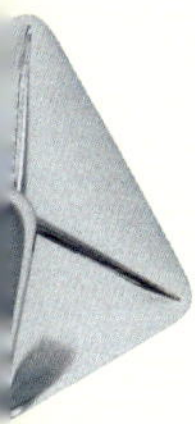

Sending the message is unlikely to go the way you want it to. Your ex might not respond as you hope they will. They might not respond at all. And you might be left feeling exposed and embarrassed and frustrated. But that doesn't mean that your feelings aren't real or valid. They really, truly are. So if you can feel the words swirling around in your mind, it's OK to get them out. In fact, it might really help. But don't send them, **OK?** Pinky swear?

44 Take a walk

This is probably the simplest solution in this book, but it's also one of the most effective. It combines the magic of moving your body (endorphins here we come) with the power of getting outside – and it doesn't require any special equipment, effort or clothing.* You don't have to go far – just around the block will suffice – but once you're underway, you'll probably find you want to keep going. Going for a walk can calm your nervous system and regulate your emotions, and it has the added benefit of physically removing you from the space you were in before, even if that space was an emotional one – so if you were tempted to text your ex, going for a walk is like literally stepping away from that mindset.

Instagram and TikTok are awash with glamorous babes going for #hotgirlwalks. If that's you, then own it. And if it's not, well, tired little potatoes are allowed to go for walks too. #tiredlittlepotatowalks

* I mean, it does require *some* clothing, unless you live in a nudist colony, but it doesn't have to be a particular *type* of clothing.

So, your fingers slipped.

WHAT TO DO IF THE TEXT HAS ALREADY BEEN SENT

First things first, **don't panic.** Everything is OK. You sent the text. You can't unsend it. I mean, even if you technically *can*, your ex will still see a note saying, 'So-and-so deleted this message', and in some ways that's worse. It's about as stealth as accidentally liking someone's Instagram post from four years ago and then just clicking 'unlike' really fast and hoping they won't notice.

You now have three options.

OPTION ONE:

Sell all your belongings, take on a new identity and move to a new country.

Perhaps a little overdramatic. This person already broke your heart, don't let them mess up your job, friendships and living situation too.

OPTION TWO:

Send a follow-up text composed largely of gibberish... wait a few minutes, then send another text saying: 'Omg, so sorry, my friend [insert suspiciously sexy sounding name here*] just grabbed my phone and sent a bunch of crazy messages to loads of people. I just had to, like, wrestle it back from them!'

I do love this option, but we both know it won't really work. Fun, though.

OPTION THREE:

Take a deep breath, put down your phone and forgive yourself.

In all honesty, this is your only real option, and I promise you it's also the best one. I know this whole book is about how you shouldn't text your ex, but you're human. We're all human. And we've all done it.

* Something like Luca or Vanessa or Jude. Or whatever tickles your pickle.

Having sent the text, you might be grappling with feelings of shame or regret or anxiety. It's OK to let yourself feel those feelings, but try not to dwell on them. You haven't done anything wrong – you're just trying to navigate a painful and challenging situation, and as much as we'd all like to approach these things with grace and poise, sometimes grace and poise abandon us and we send a Calamity Text.

Step away. Make yourself a cup of tea. Take a walk (remember how effective walking is? See page 88). Let yourself calm down. Once you feel more yourself, try journalling about it or talking it through with a friend. Name your feelings, acknowledge them, and let them go.

Recommit to focusing on yourself.

If your ex replies, it doesn't mean you have to restart a dialogue, rehash old arguments or reopen old wounds. It's OK to be honest and respond with something like, 'I probably shouldn't have sent that text. I was feeling really overwhelmed and I wasn't thinking clearly.'

Unless your ex's response to your message was: 'yea gd. U?'

In which case, honestly. Babe. Send a random and inexplicable emoji (huge fan of the dodo one, personally), then turn off your phone and go find someone who can string a sentence together.

45

Swap your phone screen for the silver screen

Take yourself out to the cinema – or the theatre, or the opera, or the ballet. Anywhere where phones are frowned upon. For this tactic, we're relying on social standards to keep us in check, so choose a film or production where there will be plenty of people in the audience to judge you if your resolve falters and you peek at your phone. Turn off your device, sit back, and immerse yourself in the story in front of you. Two or three hours will pass, you won't text your ex, and you'll get to eat popcorn. And look at that, now you have a ticket to stick in your junk journal (see page 64).

46

A stitch in time ...

... saves you from writing a Catastrophe Text.

If you've already explored the joy of cross stitch (see pages 18–19) and found the experience pleasing, then it's time to expand your horizons and adopt a new **granny hobby** (grannies are, after all, Extremely Wise). I recommend knitting or crochet. These are a little more challenging than a simple cross stitch, but they're easy to learn and you can start with something super simple, like a scarf. There is something deeply comforting about sitting with a ball of wool and some needles and watching a creation take shape before your eyes. So keep your hands busy, make something cute and enjoy your cosy new hobby.

Take your hands out of action

47

You've probably heard of the idea of adding 'friction' – barriers to keep yourself from doing things you want to avoid. In a more straightforward sense, this might look like using a screentime limit to keep yourself from spending too long scrolling, or placing your chocolate bars on a high-up shelf so you have to think a bit before you eat them all at once.

But we are currently occupying a slightly more unhinged and chaotic space, and our choice of friction needs to match that. To keep you from typing out a **Very Bad Text**, I suggest you put on a pair of mittens – or, if you have them, boxing gloves. Anything to keep you from texting. Another option is to apply so much hand cream that you can't touch anything without it slipping from your fingers – in this case, the friction comes from, ironically enough, a total lack of friction.

48 Fall in love with your neighbourhood

Leave your phone at home, buy a disposable camera and take a walk. You don't need to set out in search of a picturesque park or a stunning landscape – just mosey around your local area and look for little moments of beauty and joy, then snap away. Perhaps you'll spot a flower pushing its way through the concrete, or a striking piece of street art. Maybe you'll spot a fox nosing through a rubbish bag or spy a car with a funny registration plate. Learn to see familiar things differently, and to look more closely at the world around you. Immerse yourself in being completely where you are.

Try meditation

49

Try to calm your racing thoughts and still that texting urge by practising a little meditation. Set a timer for 5 minutes to begin with (you can increase this as you get more comfortable with meditating). Sit in a position that feels right for you: it might be cross-legged on the floor, or on a chair with your feet grounded and your back straight. Place your hands in your lap or on your knees, and close your eyes if you like. Allow yourself to breathe slowly and naturally. As you do so, focus your attention on your breath. Notice the way the way the air fills your lungs, and the sense of release as you exhale. It's natural for your thoughts to drift in this state; don't get frustrated with yourself, just notice the drifting, then bring your attention back to your breath until the timer sounds.

If you prefer, you can find a guided meditation online or using an app. However you do it, taking a few moments to calm your body and mind and just be present will help you to feel more centred and in control.

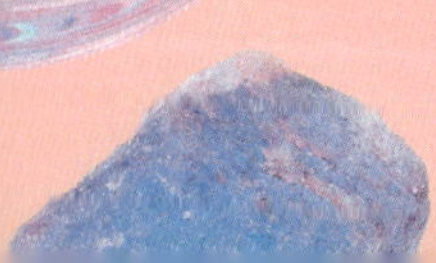

50

Get smart

If you were a high-achiever at school but have found yourself drifting away from your love of learning, this one's for you.

Humans are, by our very nature, curious and intelligent animals, and yet the way that most of our society is structured focuses on cramming all the learning into the first couple of decades of our lives, and then letting it fall by the wayside while we busy ourselves with expense reports and grocery shopping.

So stop wasting your brain power on daydreaming about bumping into your ex in the street on a day when you look extremely attractive and happy and are skipping along with a sexy new love interest, and instead use it to reignite your intellectual side. Write up a syllabus or reading list, challenge yourself to learn a new language, or do a deep dive into something you've always wanted to learn about. For bonus points, challenge some friends to do the same and then meet up and give each other presentations on what you've discovered.

AFFIRMATIONS FOR PEACEFUL SLEEP

Repeat these affirmations when your mind is racing at night.

Screentime is not me-time.

My bed is a place of calm and restoration.

I give myself permission to rest.

51

Get weighed down – in a good way

I know I keep talking about letting go of the things that are weighing you down, but sometimes being weighed down is exactly what you need. Just make sure that the thing weighing you down isn't overwhelming regret, but rather a **weighted blanket**. These heavy snuggle devices are specially designed to spread their weight evenly over you, creating a strangely reassuring pressure that can help with feelings of anxiety and overwhelm. (Also, if your hands are underneath said blanket, it's really hard to text.)

52

Dampen your enthusiasm

Desperate times call for desperate measures. If you don't have a housemate, invite a friend to stay for a few days. Give them a water pistol or spray bottle, and assure them that they have your permission to douse you liberally with water every time you mention wanting to text your ex (or if they catch you sneakily reaching for your phone). Before long, you'll associate texting your ex with the shock of icy water, and the whole thing will feel a lot less appealing.

Your most important relationship

(spoiler: it's with yourself)

This advice isn't really for the earliest days of your break-up, when you are still deep in the throes of loss and betrayal and snotty crying. It's for when you are starting to feel a little bit calmer, a little bit safer. It's for when you are taking your first baby steps back into the world, like Bambi walking on ice. I want you to think of me as your own personal Thumper.

When we're in relationships, most of us tend to devote ourselves wholeheartedly to the other person. It's not uncommon for their moods to impact our moods, for their likes and dislikes to play a role in the decisions we make, on everything from what to have for dinner to where to go on holiday. That's all pretty natural – but it's not always healthy. Compromise is an important part of a healthy relationship, and if this consideration of your partner's preferences isn't a two-way street, you can end up denying your own wants and needs in order to accommodate theirs. And that isn't good for you. It can mean you lose sight of who you really are. It's not unusual to come out of a relationship feeling a bit like you don't know yourself very well anymore. It can take a while to remember what it is that you like to do: what you like to eat, where you like to go, what the perfect night in (or out) looks like for you. Hell, you might even have trouble remembering what kind of music or TV shows you enjoy.

It's time to focus on you. To reconnect with yourself and what you want from life. It can start in small ways that might feel a bit inconsequential at first: watching those Hallmark holiday movies your ex always sneered at; setting the alarm for the time you want rather than trying to adjust your schedule to better suit theirs. But soon it will start to feel bigger. You will stretch to fill the space that they left behind – and you will fill it with yourself, and all the things that make you so uniquely who you are. You will spend your time on what matters to you. You will eat in the restaurants you want to eat in. You will talk to the people you want to talk to.

And then something magical will start to happen. You will begin to discover even more about yourself. When you give yourself just some of the attention that you devoted to your ex, you might discover passions you'd half-forgotten, or realize a new burning desire to do something you'd never even thought of (this can be where vision boards really come into their own – see pages 36–37).

It might sound like a cliché, but your most important relationship really is with yourself. You're the only one who can always be there for you, regardless of what happens. You're the person who knows yourself best. Romantic relationships, family connections and friendships are important and beautiful – of course they are. But your relationship with yourself is even more so.

It's time to start giving your time, focus and love to that relationship. **You deserve it.**

P.S. Don't text them
don't text them
don't text them.

MY PROMISE TO MYSELF...

ABOUT THE AUTHOR

Millie O'Neill is a writer and editor specializing in lifestyle and wellness. She lives in south London with two cats and an ever-growing collection of houseplants, and drinks more tea than anyone she has ever met.

Quadrille, Penguin Random House UK, One Embassy Gardens, 8 Viaduct Gardens, London SW11 7BW

Quadrille Publishing Limited is part of the Penguin Random House group of companies whose addresses can be found at global.penguinrandomhouse.com

Penguin Random House UK

Copyright © Quadrille 2026
Illustrations © Rosie Yates 2026
Stock images © Mystik Vision via Creative Market

Quadrille has asserted their right to be identified as the author of this Work in accordance with the Copyright, Designs and Patents Act 1988

No part of this book may be used or reproduced in any manner for the purpose of training artificial intelligence technologies or systems. In accordance with Article 4(3) of the DSM Directive 2019/790, Penguin Random House expressly reserves this work from the text and data mining exception.

Published by Quadrille in 2026

www.penguin.co.uk

A CIP catalogue record for this book is available from the British Library

ISBN 978 1 80712 017 7
10 9 8 7 6 5 4 3 2 1

Managing Director: Sarah Lavelle
Publisher: Kate Pollard
Commissioning Editor: Ellie Spence
Design Manager: Katherine Case
Design: Double Slice Studio
(Bonnie Eichelberger & Amelia Leuzzi)
Illustrator: Rosie Yates
Head of Production: Stephen Lang

Colour reproduction by p2d

Printed in China by C&C Offset Printing Co., Ltd.

The authorized representative in the EEA is Penguin Random House Ireland, Morrison Chambers, 32 Nassau Street, Dublin D02 YH68.

Penguin Random House is committed to a sustainable future for our business, our readers and our planet. This book is made from Forest Stewardship Council® certified paper.

FSC www.fsc.org MIX Paper FSC® C018179